Connect With Your Teen

A Workbook to Improve Communication and
Bring You Closer to Your Teen (or Pre-teen)

Candice Farrell, LMSW

Nannybird Publishing
www.nannybirdbooks.com

ISBN-10: 0615828043
ISBN-13: 978-0-615-82804-6

Cover Design By: Judith Moderacki
judithmoderacki@optimum.net
http://judithmoderacki.prosite.com

DEDICATION

This book is dedicated to my students. Thank you for all you have taught me.

Acknowledgements

My sincere appreciation and thanks to my editor Barbara Shields who generously took the time to help me and whose constant encouragement, advice and great talent immensely contributed to the final product of this book. I also want to thank Brian Shields who provided vital insight, guidance and support when I needed it most.

A special thanks to my grandmother who made an indelible impact on me, inspired me to become a teacher and instilled within me a love of writing. To my mother, Mary Ann, thank you for your sacrifices, strength, love and encouragement. I am so blessed to have you in my life. To my sisters, Kim and Christine you are the best friends I could ever ask for. Thank you for always being there. To my love, Casey, thank you for being the husband and father that you are. Your love, encouragement, patience, and understanding has made it possible for me to follow my dreams. And to my children, Sarah, Charlie and Sean whose beautiful souls inspire me to be the best person I can be. You bring so much joy into my life.

Contents

Acknowledgements v

1 Introduction: Communication Is the Name of the Game 1

2 I Have the Book, Now What? 3

3 Tips for Parents: How to Talk to Your Teen (So They'll Listen) 5

4 The Real Deal: Information for Pre-Teens and Teens 7

5 Say What!? How to Talk to Your Parents (So They Hear You) 9

6 Tell It Like It Is (Feeling Words) 11

7 My Favorites 15

8 Fun Conversation Questions 19

9 Must-Know Info: Questions About Drugs and Alcohol 45

10 So Big! Questions About Growing Up 57

11 Questions I Have and Other Stuff I'd Like to Say 73

12 You Did It! 91

References 93

1

Introduction: Communication Is the Name of the Game

Kids don't come with directions. I truly believe that the pressures of being a parent are greater than any pressure on earth. This is especially true when trying to raise an adolescent. During the pre-teen and teenage years parents and children often don't see eye to eye. I remember, when I was 11, my hamster died. I was inconsolable. My father said, "It's just a hamster. We can get another one." When I was 14, Brad Pitt first hit movie screens. I fell in love. My mother took one look at him and said, "That boy needs a haircut." But I'm getting ahead of myself.

In my decade-long role as a middle school and high school teacher, I have had the privilege of working with thousands of pre-teens, teenagers and parents, helping them stay connected. I discovered that the one quality they unequivocally share is lack of communication! In this era of texting, IM, e-mail and the internet, talking face-to-face can be an unusual experience. Many parents admit that they find out more about their child from online web pages, than from speaking to them in person. Parents are afraid they're losing touch with their children. If there's a problem, kids would rather put a message in a bottle and toss it into the ocean than talk to their parents. This workbook is designed to remedy that deer-in-headlights communication breakdown. Delve into its pages, and let it serve as a simple way of connecting and reminding each other that you care.

Communication is at the core of every human relationship. The way in which you communicate with your child establishes a foundation for him or her to build healthy, positive relationships throughout life. Research indicates that parent-child communication has a strong impact on self-image and risky behavior. Studies show that teens who reported feeling connected to parents and other family members were more likely to seek advice, facts, and confide in a parent during a time of need. They are also more inclined to delay initiating sexual intercourse, they experience less emotional distress, and are less likely to be involved in violent incidents, or have a problem with drugs. Keeping the lines of communication open and talking to your child about difficult topics can make a significant difference in his or her health and well-being.

If you are like most parents, you probably ask questions and try to reach out to your teenager, but are met with vague responses, one-word answers, or the really popular eye- rolling. Meanwhile, your kids, like many others, may be confused by the physical and emotional changes they're experiencing. Many of them are facing pressure related to sex, drugs, alcohol, school work, and just fitting in. I spend countless hours after class talking to students about what's bothering them; they often catch up with me in the hallway to ask for guidance.

When I talk to teens about the problems they're having, one of the first questions I ask is: *Have you discussed this with your parents?* I guess you know the answer to that one. While I feel honored that they trust me enough to ask my advice, it troubles me that they haven't spoken to you! Their excuses are usually the same: they're afraid of how their parents will react; that they won't understand; or, they don't want their parents to know their 'personal' business. Most fear 'getting into trouble' or losing privileges.

One of my immediate suggestions is for students to write a letter to their parent explaining the situation and their feelings. I've found that this works because it gives parents time to assess the situation before reacting, or over-reacting (as the kids say), and the outcome is typically a positive one. When I follow up with students, they are usually pleased with the results. They are more comfortable writing to their parents than having an in-person conversation and therefore feel more free to be open and honest about what is happening in their world. That is why I wrote this book. The activities will provide a fun way for you to connect, strengthen your bond, and increase the likelihood of your child turning to you in a time of need.

2

I Have the Book, Now What?

Interesting questions make for great conversations. This book provides some terrific opportunities to jumpstart fun, non-threatening dialogue that will help your child feel safe about sharing personal – and maybe even embarrassing—information with you.

The pages are divided into sections with some lighthearted and some serious questions for you and your teenager to answer. Encourage your teenager to respond to the questions he or she feels most comfortable with. The key is to make this fun for both of you. Each of you can pick and choose which questions to answer, or you can answer them all. It's up to you! Don't be afraid to open up and share your experiences with your child. Although the challenges your teenager will face in today's world are different in many ways from when you were a teen, there are also many similarities. Sharing your own personal experiences will help your child realize you can relate.

Some parents have a hard time finding the right moment to talk to their son or daughter. Open communication has a better chance of happening when you're both alone, without any other family member present. Some teens like to talk when they're sitting down to eat or at night when they are more relaxed. Many of my students complain that their parents wait until they are alone in a moving car to bring up the 'big talks.' While some kids have said they contemplated jumping out at a red light, they never do. Don't worry if it seems like your teenager isn't listening or doesn't want to hear what you are saying. My students always confess that while they may carry on and pretend they aren't listening, they do actually hear you and secretly appreciate your effort. Don't get discouraged. It may be years until your child finally admits that all your hard work was not in vain.

A student once told me that her mother put short love notes in with her lunch every day. Although the teenager referred to her mom as a 'big dork,' she revealed that she secretly cherished each one. In fact, she kept every note in a box under her bed. Whenever she needed a reminder of how much she was loved, she reached for her mom's messages and read them.

I would like to suggest that you use this book to write words of affection and encouragement to remind your child that you really care. Wouldn't it be wonderful if, decades from now, your son or daughter had this book to treasure? To recall what you value most in your life, or how he or she described their perfect day?

I've included a reference list of 'feeling' words, should you or your teenager need the perfect adjective to express how you feel. Encourage your child to be open and honest with you. Many children have learned to be people-pleasers, and as a result, they tell us what they think we want to hear. Not the truth. Let your child know that his or her thoughts, honest opinion, and point of view are important to you – even if you don't agree.

You'll notice pages at the end of the book entitled "Questions I Have and Other Stuff I'd Like to Say." You might want to use this space to ask personal questions, write special notes, discuss concerns, or even doodle sketches that express your feelings. This section might also serve as the basis for some good old-fashioned journal writing. It's up to you!

Wherever your journey takes you, it is my hope that this book will diminish the emotional distance you and your child may feel during these years, and that your child will feel more comfortable coming to you first with the problems he or she is facing. Enjoy every moment.

3

Tips for Parents:
How to Talk to Your Teen
(So They'll Listen)

Effective parent-child communication plays an essential role in the social and emotional development of your child. Here are some useful tips to keep the conversation going.

- Don't avoid the tough topics. Talking to your child openly about sex, drug and alcohol use, and other risky behaviors may discourage him or her from engaging in these activities.

- Ask open-ended questions that require more than a yes or no answer. For example, instead of asking, "Did that make you upset?" say "How did you feel when that happened?"

- Listen to the content, emotion, and intensity of what your child is expressing.

- Listen to your teenager's point of view. A child is more likely to communicate if he or she believes you understand. Children who feel that their parents hear and empathize with them often feel better about themselves.

- Try to be non-judgmental; never criticize or minimize your child's feelings.

- Acknowledge his or her emotions by saying things like, "It sounds like you were really upset."

- Let your son or daughter know you're happy that he or she opened up to you.

- Avoid accusing and/or blaming your teen. Verbalizing things like, "You always make me feel bad" or "You never do what you say you will do," causes the other person to become defensive. Instead, try to explain how you feel using "I messages." For example, say, "I feel disappointed when I ask you to do something and it doesn't get done," instead of, "You never do what I ask you to do." Open up to your child. Be honest about your own thoughts and feelings.

- Encourage your teenager to solve problems by asking, "What do you think?" or "How do you think you should handle the situation?"

- Keep in mind that sarcasm, assumptions, nagging, criticizing, lecturing, and evading questions are negative ways to communicate. It is unlikely that your child will confide in you if you let negativity get in the way.

- Become educated on the issues facing today's teens and pass that wisdom along to your child. It is better for your child to get the right information from you than to be misinformed by a friend or a kid on the bus.

- Praise opens the door to communication and boosts confidence. Try to catch your child doing something positive and praise him or her for it.

- Don't feel that you always need to fix the problem. Sometimes kids just want you to listen.

- Teenagers are trying to find their own course in life with the moral compass you've provided. They're questioning the ethical values you've instilled in them. Your job is to lead by example, and gently guide your child through the process, with love and patience. Just as you did when you were a teen, your child must decide for him or herself the importance of these morals and values.

4

The Real Deal:
Information for Pre-Teens and Teens

When I was five, I started playing softball, but I was so attached to my mother, the coach could barely get me onto the field. When I was ten, my mom would enthusiastically wave to me from the stands, and I would eagerly wave back. By the time I was 15, she was still cheering me on, but I found myself hiding in the dugout to avoid making eye contact with her. I'm not sure when things changed, they just did. My mom was as loving and supportive as always, but now that love and support, especially in a public place, humiliated me. I was sure my mother was the most embarrassing person in the world, and that she was probably trying to ruin my life. My friends thought she was sweet. So what was my problem?

I wasn't a little kid anymore, and I felt like she was still treating me like I was ten. Instead of talking to her about it, I started giving her an attitude. I rolled my eyes a lot and tuned her out. This went on for months. One day, when she finally had enough, she sat me down and demanded to know what my problem was. After a long silence, I finally blurted out that I wanted to be treated more grown-up. At that moment, an amazing thing happened---we actually started to talk! Little by little we worked things out. That day, I realized that my mother wasn't trying to ruin my life, she just didn't know how I felt or what I needed. She still came to my games, but now that crazy wave become a smile and a wink. I stopped rolling my eyes, and lost the attitude. It wasn't perfect, but we got through it.

Being a teenager isn't easy. It's the time when you get to know who you are and who you'd like to be. You may find yourself disagreeing or arguing with your parents more than you used to. And that can be frustrating. You want to run out the door, and they want to pull you back inside. You may be struggling to find more freedom, whether it's in the way you dress or how long you can stay out with your friends. You'll have highs and lows as you make difficult decisions and take on more responsibility in different areas of your life. You may feel insanely happy and terribly sad, all in the same day! You'll be stressed out, and may sometimes think no one understands how you feel. This is the time when you really have to keep the lines of communication open. You may not want to hear this, but it's important for you to turn to your parents for support and advice. Yes, advice! Your parents have a whole life of experience under their belt. It is much better to get good advice and correct information from your parents than to get bad advice or misinformation from a friend. If you are uncomfortable talking to your parents face to face about something than write it down in this book. Now is the time to ask those embarrassing questions. Just write them down!

You can also use this book to help your parents meet and get to know the grown-up you. Give them the opportunity to trust your judgment and sense of responsibility. This kind of communication can open up a whole new world for you and your parent.

5

Say What!? How to Talk to Your Parents (So They Hear You)

Here are some tips to help you communicate more effectively with your parents.

- Open up to your parents! Remember they were kids once too! Using this book together will be a learning experience for them – and for you. Although they weren't texting and using the internet when they were your age, they have a lifetime of experience in things like bullying, being pressured to use drugs and alcohol, and fitting in. Just ask them! Try talking to your parents about everyday things. Ask them how their day was or what is happening on their favorite show.

- Tell your parents how you're feeling. Don't just tell them what you think they want to hear. By being honest, you can help them see things from your point of view and earn their respect.

- It's okay to disagree, but remember to treat your mom and dad the way you'd like to be treated -- with respect.

- Listen to your parent's point-of-view. This will help you understand where he or she is coming from.

- Remember that sarcasm, assumptions, blame, criticism, and avoidance are door-slammers. That kind of negativity can break down communication between you and your parent.

- Try not to accuse or blame the other person. Think about how you'd feel if your parent said, "You always make me feel bad" or "You never do what you say you'll do." It makes him or her become defensive. Try saying something like "I felt frustrated when I wasn't allowed to go out with my friends," instead of, "You never let me do anything." Use "I messages!"

- Parents aren't mind-readers. Don't expect them to automatically know how you're feeling, or what you're thinking. That could cause a major breakdown in communication. Instead, tell them exactly what's on your mind and how you feel.

- There are times when you need to speak to a parent or adult instead of a friend. Maybe there's someone you know who's thinking about hurting himself (or maybe you are). You or a friend might be in physical or mental danger, or you may feel like you're losing control. Adults have more experience dealing with these issues and can lead you in the right direction.

- When you are writing to your mom or dad, do it when you're not distracted by TV, the computer, your phone, or other people.

- Most of all, have fun getting to know your parent better!

6

Tell It Like It Is
(Feeling Words)

It is sometimes hard to describe how you are feeling. The next two pages contain feeling words to help you better express your emotions.

Tell It Like It Is
(Feeling Words)

Accepted
Accountable
Admire
Afraid
Amazed
Angry
Annoyed
Anticipating
Anxious
Apathetic
Ashamed
Attractive
Aware

Betrayed
Bitter
Bold
Bored
Bothered
Brave

Calm
Capable
Careless
Carefree
Cautious
Cheated
Cheerful
Comfortable
Concerned
Confused
Content
Criticized

Daring
Defeated
Defensive
Depressed
Deserving
Despairing
Determined
Devoted
Disappointed

Disgusted

Eager
Ecstatic
Edgy
Embarrassed
Empathetic
Empowered
Empty
Enthusiastic
Envious
Excited
Exhausted

Fantastic
Fascinated
Fearful
Fearless
Fed up
Flustered
Foolish
Free
Frightened
Frustrated
Funny
Furious

Glad
Gloomy
Grateful
Grouchy
Grumpy
Guilty

Happy
Heartbroken
Helpful
Helpless
Hopeful
Hopeless
Hostile
Humiliated
Hurt

Impressed
Inadequate
Incredible
Independent
Indifferent
Infatuated
Innocent
Insecure
Inspired
Intimidated
Irritated
Isolated

Jealous
Joyful
Jumpy

Kind

Labeled
Liked
Lighthearted
Listless
Lonely
Loved
Lucky

Mad
Mature
Mean
Mellow
Mischievous
Miserable

Naive
Needed
Needy
Neglected
Nervous
Numb

Oblivious
Obsessed

Tell It Like It Is
(Feeling Words)

Offended
Open-minded
Optimistic

Passionate
Passive
Patient
Peaceful
Persecuted
Playful
Pleased
Preoccupied
Pressured
Protected
Protective
Proud
Provoked
Puzzled

Quiet
Quarrelsome

Reassured
Relieved
Rejected
Relaxed
Repulsed
Resentful
Respected

Sad
Safe
Satisfied
Scared
Self-conscious
Shocked
Silly
Stressed
Strong
Sympathetic

Tense
Terrified

Thankful
Thoughtful
Threatened
Tired
Troubled
Trapped

Unaware
Uneasy
Unhappy
Uninspired
Unstable
Unsure
Unwanted
Unworthy
Uplifted
Useless

Victorious
Vulnerable

Wanted
Weak
Weary
Weepy
Welcomed
Worried
Worthless

Zealous

7

My Favorites

Pages 16 & 17 include space for both of you to name your favorite things.

Favorites

Category	Parent	Teen
Movie:	_____	_____
TV Show:	_____	_____
Song:	_____	_____
Band/Artist:	_____	_____
Breakfast Food:	_____	_____
Dinner Meal:	_____	_____
Snack Food:	_____	_____
Color:	_____	_____
Radio Station:	_____	_____
Ice Cream Flavor:	_____	_____

Favorites

Category	Parent	Teen
Web Site:	_____	_____
Book:	_____	_____
Teacher:	_____	_____
Superhero:	_____	_____
Cartoon:	_____	_____
Game:	_____	_____
Place to eat:	_____	_____
Sport:	_____	_____
Place to Go With Friends:	_____	_____
Quote:	_____	_____

8
Fun Conversation Questions

Pages 20-43 include fun questions to be answered by both of you. Share the space provided.

What is the nicest thing you have ever done for someone else? Why did you do it?

One thing most people don't know about me is:

If you could travel anywhere in the world, where would it be and why?

What is your dream job?

What qualities do you look for in a friend?

What is the biggest challenge you have had to face?

What do you think are the biggest problems kids face today?

How would your friends describe you?

The most stressful thing in my life is:

What is your favorite way to spend your free time?

What is the one thing you are most afraid of?

Those who really know me know that:

What do you value most in your life?

What are the things that most annoy you?

If you could meet one person (dead or alive), who would it be? Why?

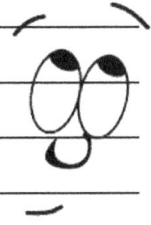

If you could trade places with anyone in the world, who would it be and why?

What is the scariest thing that has ever happened to you?

If you could change anything about the world, what would it be?

If you could change anything about yourself, what would it be?

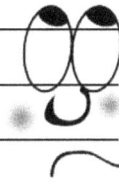

Who do you most admire? Why?

What are the 3 things you like most about yourself?

Name one thing that makes you really angry.

What qualities do you dislike in people?

Who is your biggest role model?

What have you done that you are most proud of?

What makes you happy?

Who in your life makes you feel good about yourself? Describe what they do to make you feel this way.

Who in your life would you be most likely to turn to if you had a problem? Why?

What is your favorite memory?

In 2 words, how would you describe yourself?

What is the most embarrassing thing that has ever happened to you?

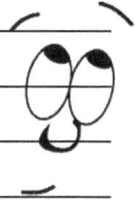

What is the most important thing you have ever learned?

What is the nicest thing anyone has done for you? Why did you think it was so nice?

What are the top 3 hopes you have for the future?

Name one opportunity you regret not taking.

I want you to know that:

What do you think is my best quality?

What do you like most about our relationship?

Name one thing I have done that most surprised you.

Is there something I can do for you that I'm not doing now?

What three words best describe our family?

If you could change one thing about our family, what would it be?

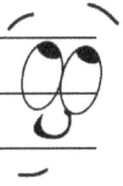

HOW will you know if you have had a successful life?

What is the best thing about our family?

9

Must-Know Info:
Questions About Drugs and Alcohol

Questions for <u>Parents</u> to Answer About
Drugs and Alcohol

What are your feelings about drug abuse?

Was drug abuse a big problem when you were my age?

What should I do if I'm ever out with friends and some-one has drugs or alcohol?

What are some things I can say to someone who is offer-ing me drugs or alcohol?

HOW would you feel if you found out I (your child) was using drugs or alcohol?

What advice do you have for me about how to handle pressure from peers to use drugs or alcohol?

Questions for <u>Parents</u> to Answer (continued)

DO you have anything else to tell me about drugs and alcohol?

Questions for <u>Kids</u> to Answer About

Drugs and Alcohol

What have you heard about drugs from your friends?

Do you know kids who use drugs or alcohol? What do you think of them?

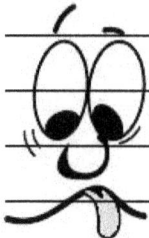

Have you ever been offered drugs or alcohol? If so, how did you handle it?

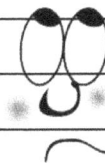

What can you do if you are out with friends and the person who is supposed to give you a ride has been drinking alcohol or using drugs?

What can you say to someone who offers you drugs or alcohol?

Why do you think someone your age would try drugs or alcohol?

If you are out with a friend who has had too much alcohol, how can you help them?

What questions do you have about drugs or alcohol?

HOW can I, as your parent, help you make good choices and stay away from drugs and alcohol?

Safety Contract

I agree to call you for advice and/or transportation at any hour, from any place, if I find myself in a situation where I feel uncomfortable, unsafe, in danger, or am impaired as a result of using drugs or alcohol.

_____

(Signature of Child)

Because I care about you, I agree to come and help you at any hour, from any place, no questions asked and no argument, to bring you home safely. We will discuss the situation together at a later time.

_____

(Signature of Parent/Guardian)

10

So Big!
Questions About Growing Up

Questions For <u>Parents</u> to Answer About
What It Was Like Growing Up

What do you remember most about your childhood?

What kind of crowd did you hang out with as a kid? Who were your closest friends growing up?

What were your parents like when you were a kid? How did you get along with them?

What kinds of things did you and your parents disagree about?

Did you ever feel left out or like you didn't fit in when you were a kid? How did you get through it?

Were you ever bullied in school? If so, how did you handle it?

What is one thing you wish you did as a teenager but never got to do?

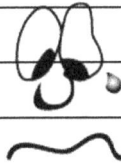

What were you like when you were my age? What kinds of things did you do for fun?

How did you do in school? What were your favorite and least favorite subjects? Why?

What kind of music did you listen to? What was your favorite artist and song?

What is one thing you know now that you wish you knew when you were young?

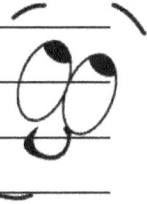

What were some of the goals you had as a teenager?

What was the most difficult problem you had to face as a teenager? How did you deal with it?

What are some similarities between you and I when you were my age?

What is your biggest wish for me?

What advice do you have for me about growing up?

Questions for <u>Kids</u> to Answer About

Growing Up

What is the best thing about being your age?

What is the hardest thing about being your age?

DO we/I have any rules that you think are unfair?

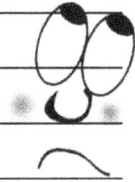

Do you ever feel like I am too hard on you?

If we could spend one day doing something together, what would you like to do?

Do you think I'm a good listener? Why or why not?

Who in your life would you be most likely to turn to if you had a problem? What is it about that person that makes you feel comfortable?

Who do you have the most fun with?

Questions for <u>Kids</u> to Answer (continued)

IS *there anything about our family that you would like to change?*

HOW *can I be a better parent to you?*

70

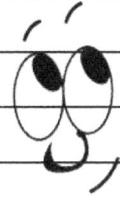

IS there anything else you would like to ask me or tell me?

11

Questions I Have and
Other Stuff I'd Like To Say...

Teens, pages 74 and 75 are for you to ask your mom or dad those personal and/or embarrassing questions you have. It is much better to get the correct information from your parents, than to get the wrong information from your friends.

Is there other stuff either of you would like to say? Pages 76-90 give you the space to write it!

Questions I have about my body:

_____

_____

_____

_____

_____

_____

_____

_____

_____

Questions I have about my relationships:

_____

_____

_____

_____

_____

_____

_____

_____

_____

_____

_____

_____

_____

Questions I have about my emotions:

_____

_____

_____

_____

_____

_____

_____

_____

_____

_____

Questions I have about sex:

_____

_____

_____

_____

_____

_____

_____

_____

_____

_____

_____

_____

_____

_____

Other stuff I'd like to say...

Other stuff I'd like to say...

Other stuff I'd like to say...

Other stuff I'd like to say...

Other stuff I'd like to say...

Other stuff I'd like to say...

Other stuff I'd like to say...

Other stuff I'd like to say...

Other stuff I'd like to say...

Other stuff I'd like to say...

Other stuff I'd like to say...

Other stuff I'd like to say...

Other stuff I'd like to say...

Other stuff I'd like to say...

Other stuff I'd like to say...

12
You did it!

Congratulations! You have finished the book! Don't let the conversation-and the fun-stop here. Continue to work on your relationship and strengthen your bond by keeping the lines of communication open. Appreciate what you love most about yourself and each other and always remember to remind one another how much you really care!

References

Advocates for Youth. (2013). Parent-Child Communication: Promoting Sexually Healthy Youth. Retrieved from www.advocatesforyouth.org

Center for Effective Parenting. (2011). How to Effectively Communicate With Your Child. Retrieved from www.parenting-ed.org

Miller, S. MD. (2013). A Letter To Parents On Teen Dataing Abuse From Pediatrician and Expert Dr. Elizabeth Miller. Love Is Not Abuse. Retrieved from www.loveisnotabuse.com

Mrug, S et al. Positive Parenting and Early Puberty in Girls: Protective Effects Against Aggressive Behavior. JAMA 2008; 162: 781-786

Resnick MD et al. Protecting Adolescents From Harm: Findings From the National Longitudinal Study on Adolescent health. JAMA 1997; 278:823-832